OCTOPUSES

BY JUDITH JANGO-COHEN

BENCHMARK BOOKS

MARSHALL CAVENDISH
NEW YORK

Dedicated to my dear Aunt Dora, whose favorite invertebrate is the butterfly, but whose second favorite is the octopus.

Series Consultant

James G. Doherty

General Curator, Bronx Zoo, New York

Thanks to Paul Sieswerda, Curator, New York Aquarium, for his expert reading of this manuscript.

The author wishes to thank Julian Whitehead of the Pittsburgh Zoo for his behind-the-scenes tour, Dr. James B. Wood

for his expert assistance, and Molly Morrison, editor.

Benchmark Books

Marshall Cavendish

99 White Plains Road

Tarrytown, NY 10591-9001

www.marshallcavendish.com

Library of Congress Cataloging-in-Publication Data

Jango-Cohen, Judith.

Octopuses / by Judith Jango-Cohen.

p. cm. — (Animals, animals)

Summary: Describes the physical characteristics, behavior, and habitat of octopuses.

ISBN 0-7614-1614-5

1. Octopodidae—Juvenile literature. [1. Octopus.] I. Title. II. Series.

QL430.3.O2.J36 2003

594'.56—dc21

2003000739

Photo Research by Anne Burns Images

Cover Photo: *Visuals Unlimited*/Shedd Aquarium, Edward Lines

All photographs in this book are used by permission and through the courtesy of:

Animals/Animals: Gregory Brown, 4; Chris McLaughlin, 9 (upper), 12–13; James Watt, 21; Breck P.Kent, 24. *Peter Arnold*: Fred Bevendam, 8 (upper),
27, 30, 35; Norbert Wu, 9 (lower), 32–33; Kelvin Aitkin, 16, 36; Jeffrey Rotman, 22. *Visuals Unlimited*: David Wrobel, 8 (center); David Fleetham, 8
(lower); Alex Kerstitch, 28. *Norbert Wu*: 9; Bob Cranston, 18 & 19. *Corbis*: Stuart Westmorland, 38; Craig Lovell, 42. Judith Jango-Cohen: 41.

Map and diagram on page 6 by Ian Warpole

Printed in China

1 3 5 6 4 2

CONTENTS

1
INTRODUCING OCTOPUSES

Two divers swim through a garden of scarlet sea fans and golden coral. A small, striped fish flits past them. One of the divers leans her hand against the coral, but quickly pulls it back. Instead of feeling sharp and hard, the coral is soft and mushy. Where her hand had been, a sleek creature rises from the coral. It turns brown, makes a smoky cloud, flashes white, and then disappears. These divers have just met an octopus.

Octopuses live in all the world's oceans. They can survive only in salt water. They may be found in sparkling tide pools with sea stars and snails, or far below the surface where it is pitch black. Some *species*, or types, cruise through ice-cold seas near the North and South Poles. Others roam the warm waters near the equator.

Scientists do not know the exact number of octopus species, but most believe there are over 150 types. One species,

AN OCTOPUS'S STICKY SUCKERS HAVE MANY USES. THEY CLING TO ROCKS AND FOOD, AND HAVE SENSORS THAT CAN FEEL AND EVEN TASTE.

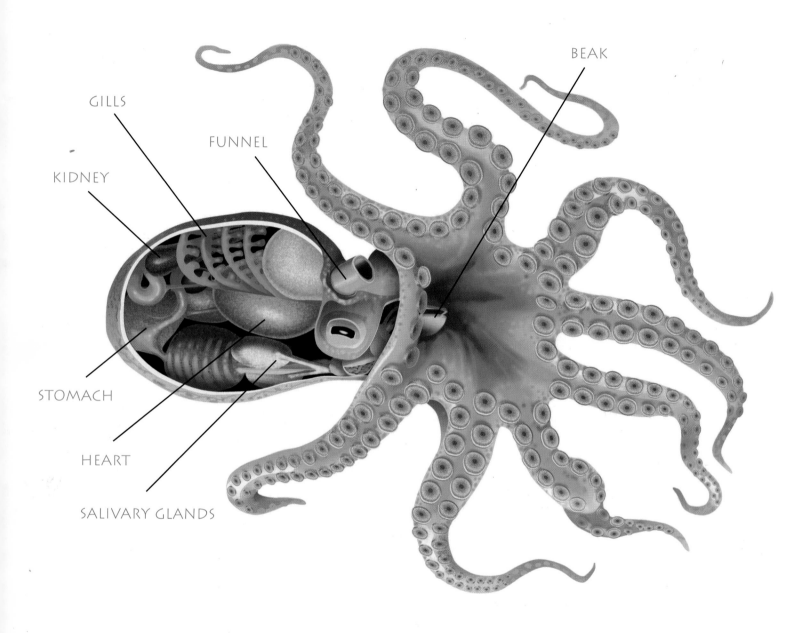

GILLS

FUNNEL

BEAK

KIDNEY

STOMACH

HEART

SALIVARY GLANDS

THIS DIAGRAM SHOWS SOME OF THE INTERNAL ORGANS LOCATED INSIDE AN OCTOPUS'S MANTLE.

the Dumbo octopus, has fins above its eyes that look like elephant ears. The dwarf octopus could be called Thumbelina. It is about the size of a child's thumb and lives in empty clamshells.

All octopus species belong to the group of animals called *cephalopods*. Other members of this group include squids, cuttlefishes, and chambered nautiluses. Cephalopods are *invertebrates*, which means they have no backbones or inside skeletons. A cephalopod's inside organs, such as the stomach, kidney, and heart, are protected by a thick covering of skin and muscle called the *mantle*. The mantle is the part of the octopus that resembles a bulging, wrinkled sack.

Cephalopod means "head foot," and that is just what an octopus looks like—a big head attached to eight feet. The eight "feet" are actually arms because they can twine around objects and grab them. These grabbing arms have a powerful grip. They are covered with circular suckers that stick like suction cups.

An octopus's suckered arms are attached around its mouth. Atop this ring of arms is the small head with two huge eyes. Behind the head is the mantle. The mantle contains the inside body organs and it has two other important uses.

OCTOPUS SPECIES

The giant Pacific is the largest octopus species. It can weigh 100 pounds (45 kg) and measure 16 feet (5 m) from mantle tip to arm tip.

Many mid-water animals, like this octopus, have transparent bodies that help them hide.

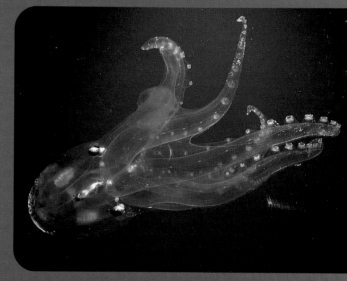

When startled, this octopus turns reddish brown with white spots.

The common octopus lives throughout the world, except in the coldest seas. It grows to about 3 feet (1 m) from mantle tip to arm tip.

This octopus from California will measure only about 1 inch (2.5 cm) long when fully grown.

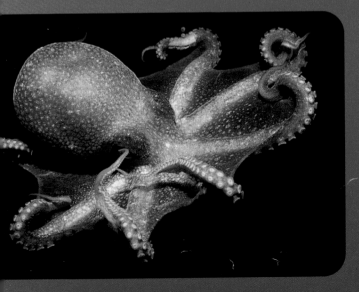

Some octopus species have webbing just at the tops of their arms. In other species, webbing extends to the arm tips.

An octopus uses its muscular mantle to breathe. By opening *mantle slits* located behind the eyes, an octopus draws in water. The water enters a space in the mantle called the *mantle cavity*. Inside the mantle cavity, two gills remove oxygen from the water. Then the slits in the mantle close, and a tube called the *siphon* opens to release the water.

An octopus also uses its mantle to swim. Tightening all its mantle muscles at once, it squeezes out a blast of water from the siphon. The thrust from the firing siphon launches the octopus. An octopus controls the force of this water to determine the speed at which it swims.

AN OCTOPUS HAS EIGHT ARMS, BUT NO **TENTACLES**. OTHER CEPHALOPODS, LIKE SQUIDS AND CUTTLEFISHES, HAVE EIGHT ARMS AND TWO TENTACLES. WHAT IS THE DIFFERENCE BETWEEN ARMS AND TENTACLES? TENTACLES ARE LONGER THAN ARMS AND HAVE BROAD TIPS. SUCKERS ARE USUALLY FOUND ONLY ON THE TENTACLE TIPS. THE RIMS OF THE SUCKERS ARE CROWNED WITH SPIKY TOPS. SOME SQUIDS ALSO HAVE HOOKS ON THEIR TENTACLES. CUTTLEFISHES AND SQUIDS SHOOT OUT THESE TENTACLES TO SNARE PASSING PREY.

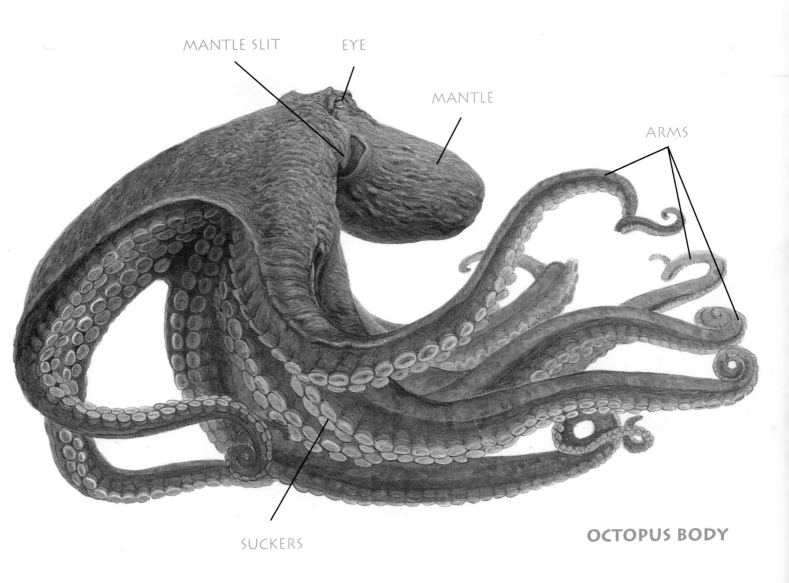

MANTLE SLIT   EYE

MANTLE

ARMS

SUCKERS

OCTOPUS BODY

OCTOPUSES HAVE A SOFT BODY AND EIGHT ARMS. EACH ARM HAS TWO ROWS OF
SUCTION CUPS. IF AN OCTOPUS LOSES AN ARM IT WILL EVENTUALLY GROW BACK.

11

A BRIAR OCTOPUS FLOATS LIKE A GHOST OVER THE SAND.

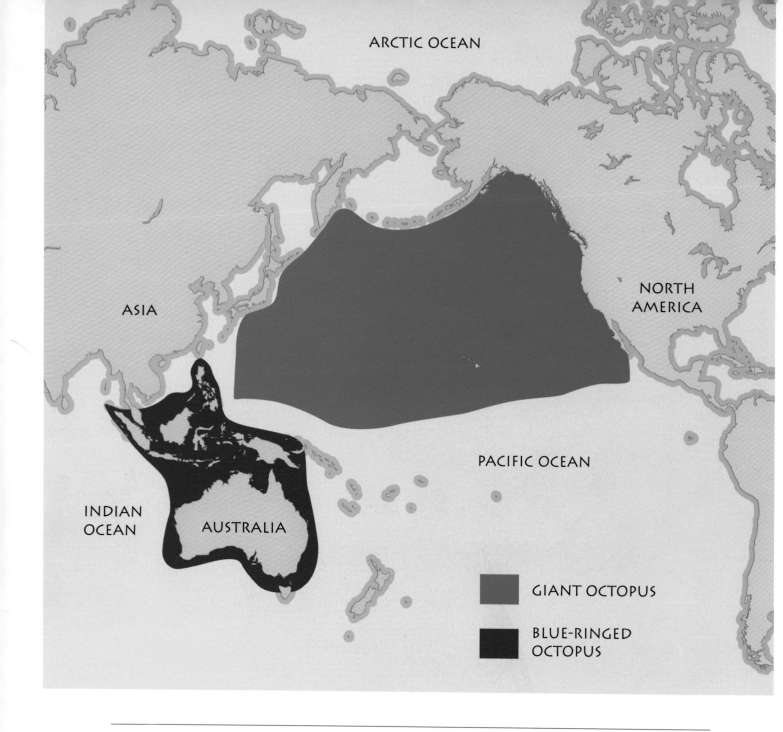

ARCTIC OCEAN

ASIA

NORTH
AMERICA

PACIFIC OCEAN

INDIAN
OCEAN

AUSTRALIA

GIANT OCTOPUS

BLUE-RINGED
OCTOPUS

THIS MAP SHOWS THE CURRENT RANGES, OR LIVING AREAS, OF TWO
OCTOPUS SPECIES.

14

An octopus can also control its direction. A backward blast of water pushes an octopus forward. A forward squirt sends it hurtling backward. Jets and rockets move this way too, using fuel instead of water.

Some octopuses give themselves an extra push with their arms. They spread their arms open, stretching the web of skin between them. Then, as a pulse of water spurts from the siphon, they flap their arms like an umbrella opening and closing.

An octopus also uses its arms for strolling along the ocean floor. As it crawls, it slowly unrolls its arms, stretching them forward. Its arms seem to dance as the octopus glides along. Suckers grip the seafloor, then relax and release as other arms reach forward. Sometimes an octopus walks with just the tips of its arms, as though it is on stilts.

Whether an octopus tiptoes through the coral or rockets away depends on why it is moving. Is it carefully searching for a meal, or trying to avoid becoming a meal for someone else?

2
DODGING DANGER

A wormlike arm squirms out from a crack in the coral. It wriggles over to a stone and curls around it. With sticky suckers, it drags the stone toward the crevice in the coral. Then the suckers release their grip and drop the rock in front of the hole. An octopus is at work. It is blockading the entrance to its den with objects such as rocks, shells, and discarded soda bottles. Hiding in a hole is one way an octopus can protect itself from *predators* such as seals, otters, sharks, and eels.

When an octopus leaves its den it has other ways to hide. Some octopuses clutch pebbles or sponge-covered shells to conceal or camouflage themselves. Others flatten their squishy bodies and wriggle into the sand. Little prickles of skin pop up to match the rough sand. When it rests against a craggy coral surface, an octopus's skin becomes even bumpier. Muscles in its skin produce these texture changes.

If becoming lumpy or smooth is not enough of a disguise,

ONLY BULGING EYES GIVE THIS HIDDEN OCTOPUS AWAY.

an octopus can change its color. It does this by opening and closing tiny sacs of *pigment*, or color, in its skin. Muscles pull tightly around the sacs, expanding them to

SCIENTISTS HAVE OBSERVED AN OCTOPUS THAT CHANGED ITS BODY PATTERN ABOUT 180 TIMES IN ONE HOUR, OR ONCE EVERY TWENTY SECONDS.

18

...BUT AS IT SETTLES DOWN, IT BEGINS TO BLEND IN WITH ITS SURROUNDINGS.

reveal the color of the pigment. When these muscles relax, the sacs shrink to tiny freckles of color. The most common pigment colors are brown, black, red, orange, and yellow. Octopuses that live in dark seas may have only brown or red pigments. Species that live in bright coral reefs may have up to five different colors.

But what if an octopus wants to blend in with a greenish,

19

seaweed–covered rock? Since it has no green pigment, it uses *reflecting cells* located underneath the pigment sacs. These cells act like mirrors by reflecting the surrounding colors. Reflecting cells also allow an octopus to match the brightness of its background. Near a very bright object, an octopus fully closes its pigment sacs, exposing all of its reflecting cells.

An octopus may seem to disappear by matching the brightness, color, or texture of its surroundings. It can also transform its skin into patches of splotches, spots, and stripes. This breaks up the outline of the octopus's body, making the octopus difficult for predators to see.

Sometimes an octopus cannot outwit a predator with its disguises. One such predator, the moray eel, hunts more by smell than by sight. Since the octopus cannot hide, it might shoot off its siphon and try to outswim the eel. The octopus

ONE TYPE OF OCTOPUS IMITATES VENOMOUS ANIMALS SUCH AS SEA SNAKES SO PREDATORS WILL STAY AWAY. THIS OCTOPUS WILL STICK SIX ARMS INTO A HOLE AND WAVE THE OTHER TWO LIKE SWAYING SNAKES. TO COMPLETE THE IMITATION, IT CHANGES COLOR TO BLACK-AND-YELLOW STRIPES.

THIS OCTOPUS APPEARS TO BE NAPPING IN KONA, HAWAII.

WITH A BILLOWING INK CLOUD, AN OCTOPUS VANISHES.

may also release a burst of dark ink from its siphon. This swirling cloud of ink confuses the eel, giving the octopus more time to escape.

An octopus can create a floating shape that resembles itself by mixing mucus with the ink. A predator will often attack this decoy, while the real octopus slips away. Experiments show that the inky mixture may also interfere with a predator's sense of smell.

3
A CUNNING HUNTER

An octopus hides beside a boulder. As still as a stone, it waits for lunch. A little crab hobbles by, heading for a patch of seaweed. The watchful octopus reaches out a curled-up arm and unwinds it toward the crab. Then it taps the crab with its arm tip and reels in the meal stuck to its suckers. An octopus's suckers have sensors that can feel and even taste the crab.

Hiding is a great way to catch *prey*, but when an octopus is hungry it may also go hunting. Crawling over the sand, it pokes its arm tips into holes and cracks. It is feeling and tasting for hidden prey like fish, shrimp, snails, clams, and crabs.

Sometimes an octopus uses the webbing between its arms to capture prey. An octopus's arms are webbed, or connected, at the base. Pouncing on a rock, the octopus smothers the stone in its cape-like arms. Then it rolls the rock over and snatches whatever is hiding underneath.

CRABS CANNOT ESCAPE THE STRONG TUG OF THESE SUCKERS.

If an octopus finds its prey out in the open, it may rev up its siphon and race toward it. Then, spreading its arms, the octopus floats down and nets the animal.

Some octopuses must find food in the dark depths of the sea. One species of deep-sea octopus has solved this problem by luring its prey. Its blue-green, glow-in-the-dark suckers attract swarms of tiny creatures. Scientists think these creatures get stuck in the mucus around the octopus's mouth. This makes for easy eating.

Most of the creatures an octopus eats come in shells. These can be difficult to open. An octopus may use its suckers to pull apart animals called *bivalves*, which include oysters and clams. It can also crack lobster or crab shells with its parrotlike beak. When an octopus is not eating, the beak is tucked inside its mouth. The tongue is covered with teeth that are used to scrape holes in shells.

Saliva, or spit, also plays a part in how an octopus eats. While drilling holes in shells, the common octopus spits out saliva. The saliva contains a substance that assists in

OCTOPUSES HAVE TO WATCH WHAT THEY SWALLOW. A NARROW FOOD TUBE, WHICH CONNECTS MOUTH TO STOMACH, PASSES DIRECTLY THROUGH THE OCTOPUS'S BRAIN. SCIENTISTS HAVE FOUND BITS OF SWALLOWED SHELL PIECES STUCK IN THE BRAINS OF SOME OCTOPUSES.

AN OCTOPUS COLLECTS A FEW CRABS AND BRINGS THEM BACK TO ITS DEN TO EAT.

THE VENOMOUS BLUE-RINGED OCTOPUS FLASHES ITS RINGS WHEN ALARMED.

wearing away the shell. Other substances in octopus saliva soften the prey's body and break down attachments to the shell. The soft body falls cleanly away from the shell, allowing the octopus to retrieve every morsel.

Breaking into shells is not an octopus's only feeding

dilemma. Sometimes it has to deal with snapping crab or lobster claws. The saliva is useful for this problem too. *Venom* in the saliva paralyzes prey, allowing the octopus to eat in peace. Octopuses also inject bivalves with this venom. A paralyzed bivalve can no longer clamp its shells together.

Before dining, an octopus often brings its prey back to the den. After eating, it blows out the litter of empty shells with its siphon. It also blows away little fishes that pester it for scraps.

IF YOU ARE IN AUSTRALIA YOU MAY SEE A BLUE-RINGED OCTOPUS. IT WOULD FIT IN YOUR HAND, BUT DO **NOT** PICK IT UP! WHEN DISTURBED, THE BLUE-RINGED OCTOPUS MAY FLASH ITS RINGS AND ATTACK. ITS VENOMOUS BITE CAN KILL YOU. THE VENOM PARALYZES MUSCLES— INCLUDING THE MUSCLES THAT HELP YOU BREATHE. SOME PEOPLE WHO HAVE BEEN BITTEN HAVE SURVIVED WITH THE HELP OF MOUTH-TO-MOUTH RESUSCITATION OR BREATHING MACHINES. THE VENOM USUALLY WEARS OFF IN ABOUT TWENTY-FOUR HOURS.

4
BATCHES OF HATCHLINGS

A common octopus curls up in a snug, rocky hollow. Swirling an arm overhead, she fastens a tiny tasseled chain to the ceiling. For two weeks, she has been hanging dozens of these pretty, glittering strings. The octopus is not decorating her den. These pearly strands are actually made up of thousands of her eggs. Each egg has a stem. By twisting the stems together, the common octopus makes a dangling chain.

Not all octopuses create these egg necklaces. Species that lay fewer and larger eggs glue their eggs up one by one. Octopuses that live on flat, sandy seafloors, where there are not many rocky shelters, have no place to attach their eggs. These species carry clusters of eggs under their webs. One devoted octopus mother was discovered carrying 36,000 eggs, which totaled nearly half her own weight. No matter how a female octopus lays her eggs, she will lay only one batch of eggs in her lifetime. Mother octopuses die soon after their eggs hatch.

LARGE EYES PEER FROM SEE-THROUGH EGGS.

THIS TWO-SPOTTED OCTOPUS CRADLES A CLUTCH OF EGGS.

Once an octopus lays her eggs she must protect them until they hatch. Little fishes lurk outside her den in hope of snatching the group of eggs, called a *clutch*. Crabs and shrimp would eagerly feast on the eggs if the mother left her post. The octopus also protects her eggs by "dusting" them with her nimble arm tips. Carefully, she wipes away dirt and tiny *parasites*. She also keeps oxygen circulating around the eggs with gentle puffs of clean water from her siphon.

Meanwhile, the young common octopuses are busily growing in their soft, see-through eggs. Two huge eyes appear. Pigment sacs open and close like blinking lights. Almost three months later, the eggs jiggle and jump. The young are ready to hatch. They plop from their eggs like dripping water droplets. With pulsing squirts from their siphons, the babies bounce around in the water.

Some newly hatched octopuses settle immediately on the bottom and go about their business of hiding and feeding. This is true for the dwarf octopus, which lays small batches of large eggs. These well-developed hatchlings

OCTOPUSES LIVE ONLY A FEW YEARS. THE COMMON OCTOPUS HAS A LIFE SPAN OF TWELVE TO EIGHTEEN MONTHS. THE GIANT PACIFIC OCTOPUS LIVES BETWEEN THREE AND FIVE YEARS.

A GIANT PACIFIC OCTOPUS GUARDS THE EGG CHAINS THAT ARE GLUED TO ITS DEN.

BLUE-RINGED MOTHERS CARRY THEIR EGGS UNTIL THE BABY OCTOPUSES HATCH.

look like miniature adults. They have long arms and can crawl and hunt along the bottom.

Other species, like the common octopus, lay massive clutches of tiny eggs. These hatchlings are not as well developed. Their stubby arms are even shorter than their bodies. These young octopuses must drift on the surface of the sea where they can capture other tiny floating organisms.

Wherever they wind up after they hatch, most octopuses will be snapped up and gulped down by other hungry creatures. But a few lucky ones will survive. By cleaning her clutch, supplying oxygen-rich water, and chasing off egg-eating predators, the female octopus does her best to ensure that life will continue.

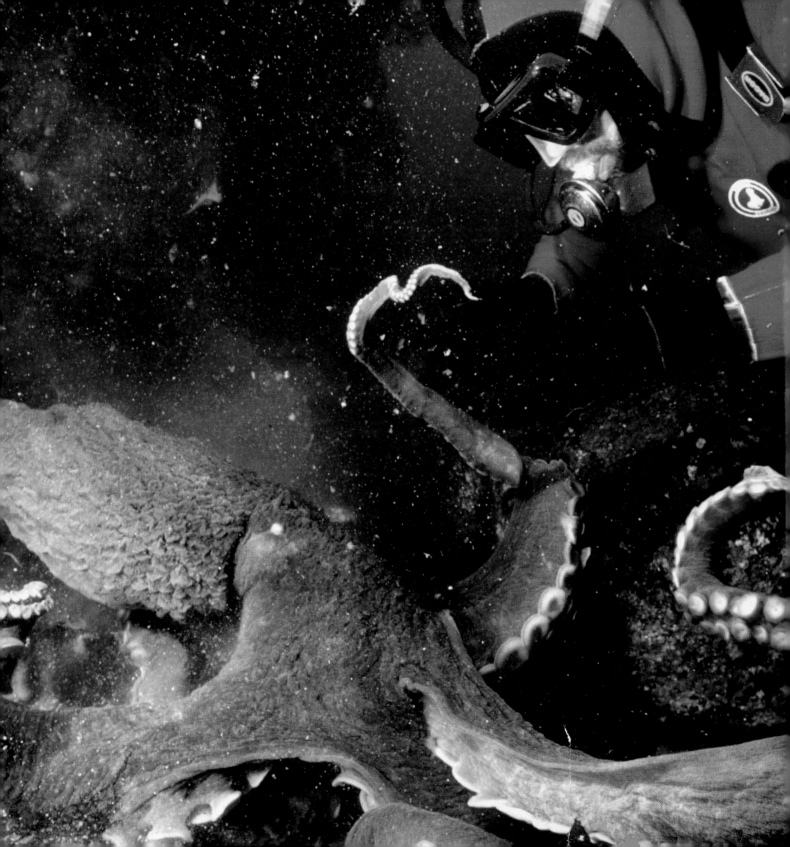

5
OCTOPUSES AND US

At the New England Aquarium in Boston, a giant Pacific octopus is pressed against its glass tank. It looks like a glob of modeling dough. SPLASH! A hand slapping the surface of the water lets the octopus know it is mealtime. Down comes an anchovy speared on the tip of a pole. The octopus eats the little fish and two others. Then it drifts casually to the top of the tank.

A staff member takes hold of two of the octopus's arms, drawing the animal to him. The 15-pound (7 kg) octopus explores the man's hands and bare arms, tasting and feeling with its suckers. The octopus is cold and slippery and has a strong, muscular grip. When the man removes the suckered arms from his own, there are loud SNAPS! like the popping of bubble wrap.

Looking after this seven-month-old octopus requires more than just feeding it. To keep the octopus stimulated and alert, the aquarium has developed an enrichment

A GIANT PACIFIC OCTOPUS ALLOWS A DIVER TO APPROACH.

program. Sometimes staff members give it vinyl puppy toys to examine. The octopus also explores a toy tower of plastic rings. It removes the rings from a pole and passes them around to its other arms.

The staff also challenges the octopus with clear plastic cubes containing crabs. Each cube has a different type of lock. Some locks need to be turned, while others have to be pushed. At first the octopus may take half an hour to open the lock. But as the octopus learns, it reaches its food faster. When the octopus becomes an expert, staff members stack different cubes inside each other. During one feeding session the octopus ignored the locks. Instead, with its suckered arms, it yanked off one side of the cube.

The curiosity and intelligence of the octopus can cause problems. Octopuses sometimes squeeze their mushy bodies through tiny cracks in tank covers. Then they may visit other tanks, making nighttime snacks of their neighbors. Divers have run into problems with octopuses that have

SCIENTISTS HAVE OBSERVED OCTOPUSES PLAYING WITH A FLOATING PILL BOTTLE, REPEATEDLY BLASTING IT WITH WATER FROM THEIR SIPHONS. THIS MADE THE BOTTLE CIRCLE THE TANK AND RETURN TO THEM LIKE A BOUNCING BALL.

EMERGING FROM THE WATER, AN OCTOPUS GREETS ITS KEEPER.

JACQUES COUSTEAU FOUND OCTOPUSES TO BE SHY, PLAYFUL, AND INTELLIGENT.

grabbed at their masks and cameras. If the diver struggles, the octopus may get nervous and tighten its grip. But usually, when the octopus's curiosity is satisfied, it lets go.

Jacques Cousteau, the famous oceanographer, once brought a giant Pacific octopus aboard one of his research vessels. He placed it in a small, covered tank with several 20-pound weights holding the top closed. The octopus managed to raise and remove the cover. One by one, its arms squirmed out of the tank. Then its eyes appeared. Finally, its whole body oozed over the edge of the tank and splattered onto the deck and overboard. Back in the sea, the octopus turned strong and sleek. With a swirl of ink, it streaked away.

bivalves: Animals that have two shells held together by a hinge, like a scallop or clam.

cephalopods: The group of more than 600 marine invertebrates with soft bodies, mantles, large brains, large eyes, beaks, siphons, and long, flexible arms.

clutch: A group of eggs laid by an animal.

invertebrates: Animals without backbones, such as insects, crabs, snails, and octopuses.

mantle: The muscular covering located behind the head that encloses a cephalopod's internal organs.

mantle cavity: The water-filled space inside the mantle that contains the gills.

mantle slits: Openings in the mantle that allow water to enter the mantle cavity.

parasites: Organisms that live, grow, and feed on other organisms.

pigment: Substance that gives color to a plant or animal's body.

predator: An animal that hunts and eats other animals.

prey: An animal that is hunted and eaten by other animals.

reflecting cells: Structures beneath the pigment sacs that reflect light, allowing an octopus to blend in with the brightness and color of its surroundings.

saliva: The fluid in the octopus's mouth containing venom that paralyzes prey and substances that wear down shells and partly digest food.

siphon: Tube that expels water from the mantle cavity, used for breathing and for swimming.

species: A particular type of plant or animal.

tentacles: The two specialized arms that squids and cuttlefishes use to capture prey.

venom: Poison of some snakes, spiders, and other animals that is passed to another animal by a bite or a sting.

BOOKS

Carrick, Carol. *Octopus*. New York: Clarion, 1978.

Cerullo, Mary M. *The Octopus: Phantom of the Sea*. New York: Dutton, 1997.

Hirschi, Ron. *Octopuses*. Minneapolis: Carolrhoda Books, Inc., 2000.

Hunt, James. *Octopus and Squid*. Monterey: Monterey Bay Aquarium Foundation, 1996.

llamas, Andreu. *Octopuses: Underwater Jet Propulsion*. Milwaukee: Gareth Stevens Publishing, 1996.

Martin, James. *Tentacles: The Amazing World of Octopus, Squid, and Their Relatives*. New York: Crown Publishers, Inc., 1993.

Stephens, William and Peggy. *Octopus Lives in the Ocean*. New York: Holiday House, 1968.

MAGAZINES

Bavendam, Fred. "Eye to Eye with the Giant Octopus." *National Geographic*, March 1991: 86–97.

Schleichert, Elizabeth. "Eight-armed and Awesome!" *Ranger Rick*, February 2000: 2–9.

Voss, Gilbert. "Shy Monster, the Octopus." *National Geographic*, December 1971: 776–799.

VIDEOS

The Octopus. Diamond Entertainment, 1996.

The Undersea World of Jacques Cousteau: Octopus-Octopus. Pacific Arts Video, 1986.

WEBSITES

FIND OUT MORE

The Cephalopod Page

Dr. James B. Wood

http://is.dal.ca/%7Eceph/TCP/index.html

Monsters of the Deep

http://www.abc.net.au/science/ocean/monsters/default.htm

Nature: The Octopus Show

http://www.pbs.org/wnet/nature/octopus/index.html

Octopus!

Anne Worrall

http://projects.edtech.sandi.net/encanto/octopus/index.htm

Octopus Studies

Dr. Mark Norman

http://www.australiancephalopods.com/index_octopus.htm

ABOUT THE AUTHOR

Judith Jango–Cohen first wrote about the octopus when she was in fourth grade and has been intrigued by them ever since. Recently she had the opportunity to go behind the scenes at the New England Aquarium in Boston. There she observed and photographed their giant Pacific octopus. Photographing and watching the octopus with Jango–Cohen was her husband Eliot. They live in Burlington, Massachusetts with their children, Jennifer and Steven. To find out more about their books and photography, see www.agpix.com/cohen.

INDEX

Page numbers for illustrations are in **boldface.**